Thoughts from Abroad

Simon Acland

THE CAXTON PRESS

ISBN 1-877303-05-4

First Printed August 2006

Printed & Published by The Caxton Press, Christchurch, New Zealand
Distributed in New Zealand by Nationwide Book Distributors Ltd.
30 Stewart Street, Christchurch

For my mother

and in memory of

Brian Ward

acknowledgements

None of this could have happened without Radio New Zealand. It all began with Grace Green who invited me to recite a poem on 3ZB Children's Hour when I was six. The late Dianne Stogre Power, a producer with Radio New Zealand, encouraged me but it was Elizabeth Alley, then Programme Development Manager who gave me my first contract and the confidence to continue. I am most grateful to her for the foreword to this book. Paul Bushnell, Features Manager at Radio New Zealand, kept me on after Elizabeth retired and has continued to give me support and guidance. I am grateful as well, to friends, family and especially to those National Radio listeners who have popped up everywhere from the main street in Geraldine, South Canterbury, to a jungle path in Cambodia and who have commented favourably on my broadcasts. Deborah Nation, my producer has been a good friend and a tough critic without whose advice and expertise I would have found it impossible to keep going. She and John Boardman have been enthusiastic about this book. John has added to that enthusiasm his editing and literary skills for which I am hugely grateful as I am for his constant support throughout this project.

Simon Acland 2006

foreword

While travelling in Europe last year, we often had cause to reflect on how the nature of travel has changed. It's not just that there are so many more people doing it. Nor is it even much to do with the disappearance of the frontiers of travel because the most interesting places are now mapped and documented in a way that diminishes the spirit of personal adventure and makes the world seem so much smaller. What really hits you is that while travel may still broaden the mind, it is also narrowing the vision. Many no longer see things the way they once used to. Battalions of travellers uniformed by their guides into fluorescent-jacketed identification, raced through European streets shepherded by umbrella-wielding tour leaders. Their gaze was fixated not on the art or the architecture, but on the viewfinder of the digital camera. In Venice, gondolas slid through gleaming canals walled by buildings of classical beauty and historical significance, while their enraptured cargo fixed a blinkered gaze on the digital square. Vaporettos carried tourists whose right arms extended in some kind of universal digital salute, thereby missing all but a miniaturized view of that grand and architecturally magical city. It gave a new meaning to 'thinking outside the square.'

Simon Acland doesn't use a camera. His tools of observation are his eyes and ears. To the images he captures in a manner far more graphic than mere photography, he adds his genuine interest and warm compassion for his fellow man, with a refreshing absence of judgementalism. With the heightened insight of the committed and experienced traveller, he finds his inspiration from simple human exchange and everyday incident, delighting in cultural difference and finding good where it may not always be immediately apparent. He is an observer with a natural curiosity about the diverse characteristics that comprise the huge mosaic of the human condition. He is able to open up conversational possibilities not always available to everyone–people tell him things. Like all good travellers he's alert to the nuances of speech or gesture – a glance between two people or a quiet exchange can lead him towards an incident from which we can draw some kind of personal meaning. Most of all, he has an intuition for a good story and an ability to tell it in a way that reaches beyond the event itself, to give it wider relevance and deeper significance to our daily lives.

When he and his producer Deborah Nation first approached me at Radio New Zealand with the idea that became the occasional National Radio series Thoughts from Abroad, on which this selection is based, it was at a time when we wanted to develop what might be called 'values-based' programming. There was a need for material that enabled listeners to relate their own ethical or moral beliefs to everyday issues and real-life stories based on social, moral and human concerns outside traditionally religious frameworks. Such was the positive response to these pieces, that they became an anticipated and regular part of holiday listening. Listeners and readers are able to interpret them in whatever way is most helpful–some are pieces of wide general interest to any concerned citizen of the world, others may carry a deeper religious message. Collectively they inform, often amuse, always interest and sometimes provoke us into broader thinking. Most of all, they are human vignettes of universal meaning which help us make sense of our own place in an increasingly complex world.

Elizabeth Alley
Wellington 2006

contents

a prince on the underground

I know that you don't speak to people on the tube, the London Underground. I knew it when I first went to London in the 1960's. After a couple of weeks there, I'd at least learned that. Then my mother arrived for a visit from New Zealand and was staying in my flat. She'd been to London before and she certainly knew that you don't speak to strangers on the Underground.

We were at Notting Hill underground station waiting for a train to Oxford Circus when further down the platform my mother saw a tall, distinguished looking African in tribal robes with great feathers in his headdress. Not a common sight in those days.

'Who's that?' she asked me.

I thought it was Prince Monolulu. I'd seen his photo in the papers and had read that he was a racing tipster. His popular cry was, 'I gotta horse!'

‘What’s a racing tipster?’ my mother asked. I didn’t know. Then she said, ‘I’m going to ask him.’

I was horrified. ‘No, Mum you can’t. You don’t talk to people on the tube.’

‘We’re not on the tube,’ she said. ‘We’re on the platform.’

Of course, strictly speaking she was right, but the same rule applied and she knew that perfectly well. Fortunately, a train came in at that moment and I hoped that might be the end of the matter. It wasn’t! As it turned out, we got into the same carriage as Prince Monolulu. I went at once to the other end and tried to keep out of sight. My mother, of course, went straight up to where the Prince was sitting and said, ‘I’m Mrs Acland from New Zealand. My son, who’s hiding down there at the other end of the carriage, tells me that you are Prince Monolulu and that you are a racing tipster. Do tell me. What is that?’

At this, the Prince turned to the person sitting next to him and said, ‘Stand up. Give the lady a seat.’ The man stood, my mother sat, and Prince Monolulu told her about horse racing.

My mother turned to the person on her other side and said, ‘Isn’t that fascinating. I never knew that. Did you?’ Whereupon, someone sitting opposite said, ‘My cousin went out to New Zealand six years ago, to somewhere called Nelson. I wonder if you’ve met her?’ And another person began to talk about a sister who was in Sydney and who was trying to work out whether to visit New Zealand or not.

By the time we reached Oxford Circus you would have thought that we were at a very lively party. I was still standing at the end of the carriage, self conscious and embarrassed but with a degree of admiration for my talkative mother. Only we hadn’t been at a party. We’d been on the Central Line. As we left the train, everyone called out to say, ‘Goodbye,’ and ‘Have a good time in London.’ We’d been on the London Underground where nobody talks to anyone!

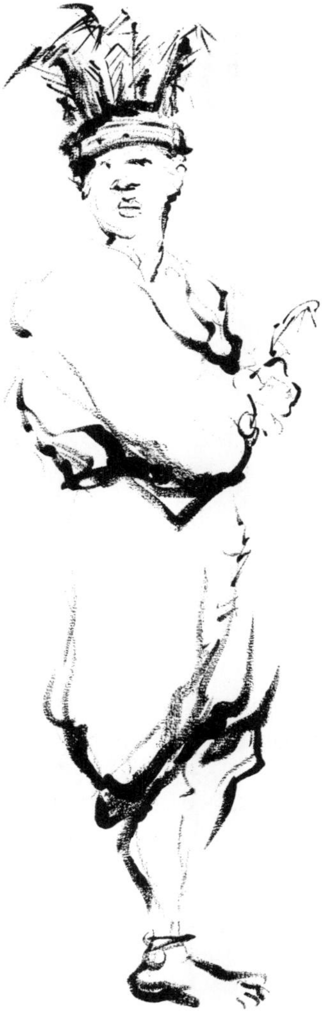

the child is father of the man

A good friend of mine, Brian Ward, died not long ago. He was only 72 and generally very healthy but there was some heart defect and after three massive operations he died. He is survived by an elder brother.

I helped as best I could with the formalities of registering the death and I organised the cremation and the Service of Thanksgiving that followed.

Inevitably his brother and I talked a good deal about Brian and I discovered as much if not more about him after his death than I had known before: different things, more about the distant past than about recent years. One of the things that interested me was why Brian had chosen to live and work in South East Asia - in Malaysia, in Indonesia but chiefly in Thailand. In fact for thirty years, more than half his working life, he lived and worked in Asia.

His brother thought that maybe it was because after Brian retired from twenty years' service in the British regular army he took a year off and 'for fun' had driven through the Middle East and Asia by car. During that year he fell in love with Asia and never really left.

Brian's work was in assisting Asian countries create the systems to deal with disaster preparedness and disaster management. He was good at his work and hugely respected for it.

After the services in London I was asked to go to Bangkok to liaise with the Buddhist monks who would conduct the ceremonies there after which I was to commit his ashes to the waters of the Gulf of Thailand. Brian's instructions were that his ashes were to be 'dumped' into the Gulf of Thailand. He was a practical man.

A few days afterwards, his brother who was still sorting through Brian's personal effects called me. He said he had something to tell me and something to show me. He had found a piece of paper.

He told me that when they were boys, he nine and Brian six, they attended a small primary school in Hampstead, North London. Their father was a surgeon and reasonably well to do. Each Sunday they were allowed to invite a friend home for tea. This was pre war Englandwith old-fashioned courtesies and customs.

'We each had our pals we would invite,' the brother told me. 'And the odd thing was, odd for those days anyway, my brother's special pal was a Chinese boy called Lung.'

There would have been very few Asians living in Hampstead at that time, perhaps families of diplomats, but certainly Lung was the only Asian at that small school.

The brother told me that he had been going through a box in which were my friend's most important and most personal papers. 'And,' he said, 'I found this.'

He showed me a piece of paper. On it was drawn a picture of a ship, a man-o-war in full sail with canons along the side. A child's drawing. A boy's drawing. And written along the top in pencil and then over the pencil in ink, 'Lung drew this and is aged 7.'

'That is undoubtedly Brian's childhood hand,' his brother said. 'Now you have the answer to why he devoted the greater part of his life to helping the people of Asia. Indeed the child is father of the man.'

the nanny state

Thank goodness I stopped smoking fourteen years ago now - mainly because of my health. I was wheezing when I went up the stairs. And there was the cost as well. Today, there would be so many places from which I'd be banned, glared at and disapproved of. All that guilt inducing stuff would be enough to drive me to drink or to take up smoking. Evidently, the new legislation in the UK is going to deal with the smoking issue once and for all.

Then in the British press, earlier in the year it was all about 'obesity'. A government paper. Horror stories about overweight children and adults. Then legislation and threats of more legislation. Well, I was ahead of that one too. Four years ago, after some seriously careful eating over a period of more than six months, I lost three stone.

The next issue was smacking children, or rather not smacking them. My children are all over the age of twenty four so smacking is not a consideration. Smacking was debated in the House of Lords with strong feeling on all sides. Amendments to the legislation proposed, opposed, debated.

Of course it goes without saying that smoking, obesity and smacking can have appalling results. But somewhere in the midst of all the debating, I do wonder about the usefulness of more and more state legislation as the way to solve these problems. I gather it's called the Nanny State.

Now that simply won't do. We all know that New Zealand nannies are the best in the world.

And the last thing a good New Zealand nanny will do is to mollycoddle the children, tut tut continuously, or go on making new rules to control them. A good New Zealand nanny recognises that children will make mistakes. They'll fall off their tricycles. They'll fall onto the concrete. The good nanny will help the children to learn from their mistakes and to grow up learning to be independent and responsible and able to make their own decisions, even if they are wrong.

Call controlling, tut tutting governments something else by all means but no more of this 'Nanny' state. It's an insult to good New Zealand nannies.

on the train to pisa airport

I was in Italy, in a train, on my way to Pisa airport. I got on at Lucca – it's about half way between Florence and Pisa. A young American – backpack and all of that – was sitting there and he said to me, 'Is this Pisa?'

'No, it's Lucca,' I said.

'Oh. I'm sorry. I don't speak Italian,' was his puzzling response. I told him I didn't either and it turned out he was a student from Iowa in the United States and that he was studying German for a year, in Austria. He was going to Pisa, he told me, to see the leaning tower.

But what he really wanted to tell me was that the night before he'd been to the Paul McCartney concert in Rome. There had been over 200,000 people and it was in the Colosseum, he said. He'd queued for over 24 hours and he had a seat in the fifth row.

Everything about the concert was wonderful. It was the

most fantastic event in his life. 'I never dreamt I would actually see and hear Paul McCartney himself, the real one. I have. And today I'm wiped out.'

'So,' I asked him, 'What did you do after the concert?'

'Well, I went to the railway station but it was closed. I wanted to come to Pisa today so I found a corner near the station and went to sleep there with my head on my backpack. I woke up about three hours later. Everything was strewn everywhere. My clothes were all around me. The backpack was still under my head but empty. My digital camera was gone. It was worth 400 dollars and I'm really pissed off about the photos.'

'But,' he continued, 'I had $98 tucked into my underpants and they didn't get that. Do you know they somehow stole my passport out of my pocket while I slept.'

'This is terrible,' I said.

To which he replied, 'Oh, yeah. But I've seen Paul McCartney.'

mount athos

Mount Athos is a peninsula in northern Greece stretching south into the Aegean Sea. It is only eight kilometres wide and just over fifty six kilometres in length. For more than a thousand years, it has been home to Orthodox Christian monks. In the 1960's, it seemed as though monasticism was finished. The number of monks had dwindled and those who were left were elderly.

Today, there are more than 2000 monks and their numbers are continuing to grow. They come from Bulgaria, Romania, Russia and Serbia as well as Greece and there are converts from Western Europe, Great Britain and America.

Mt Athos is called the 'holy mountain' and is unique in that it is a bit of Europe dedicated to the monastic life and to nothing else. Tradition has it that the holy mountain was visited by the Blessed Virgin Mary and for that reason it is dedicated to her. All other women are excluded from it. The Orthodox believe that it is indeed holy ground.

The first time I visited Mt Athos, I went by bus from Thessalonica to Ouranapoulis, caught a boat to the fishing port of Daphni then travelled again by bus to Karyes, the capital city but really little more than a small town. I walked down Holy Ghost Street, had my permit stamped, then returned to Daphni to catch the launch to the monastery that I was to visit.

The launch deposited me at the jetty and left. The Monastery of Simon Peter is high up on the cliff and to get to it from the coast you must walk up a narrow path cut into the cliff face. But even before I started my walk, I saw a sign at the end of the jetty. It read in English, French and German: 'Pilgrim Welcome'. Then underneath: 'You are not welcome after midday. You are not welcome unless previous arrangements to visit the monastery have been made.' It was three in the afternoon. I had made no arrangements, it was blazingly hot and the launch had gone.

There was no alternative. I started walking up the path. About a third of the way up, enjoying the sun on the path ahead of me was a very large snake. Now, I don't know much about snakes but I know that I don't like them. I didn't know there were snakes in Greece. I associate them more with the jungle. But there it was. I waited. It didn't move. I nervously kicked a pebble at it. It moved a little further up the path. I waited again and kicked another pebble. After what seemed to me a very long time, the snake clearly realised that it wasn't going to be able to sleep uninterrupted in the sun. It slithered off the path and down the cliff.

On I went, pouring with sweat. About two thirds of the way up the path, for no apparent reason, one of the lenses fell out of my glasses and smashed on the rocks. I'm as blind as a bat without my glasses. There was no alternative but to hug the cliff face and stumble onwards and upwards.

Eventually, I reached the monastery and the monk guest master could not have been more welcoming. I was taken to a spotlessly clean dormitory and then shown the chapel. I was also shown where the showers were - only cold water but much appreciated none the less. The guest master gave me bread, olives and raki, a fiery alcohol - the pilgrim's welcome.

Later, another of the monks came to talk to me. He spoke English and followed the Orthodox custom of introducing a subject and then allowing me to ask a question which he would then answer. This was not a time for chat or a discussion.

He spoke to me about the Orthodox understanding of the Holy Spirit and of how God inhabits the whole world. If we would only open our eyes, we could see the working of God in everything that happens. 'For example,' he continued, 'if a tile fell from this roof and hit me on the head, then I should try to understand what God is saying to me in this. Similarly, of course, if the tile missed me, I should try to understand that.'

I then told him of my arrival, the notice on the jetty, the snake and my broken spectacles.

'Oh yes,' he said. 'But you must recognise that for the pilgrim there are always obstacles to be overcome.' I expressed some surprise at this interpretation and wondered whether I shouldn't have been obedient to the instructions on the jetty notice. He was silent. It wasn't my place to answer my own questions. If I did, why had I asked the question in the first place?

'And the serpent,' he said. I had said 'snake'.

'There is always sin to be overcome.' This time I was silent.

'And the broken spectacles.' And with a faint smile he continued, 'The blindness of the Western Church perhaps?'

We talked a lot. The thing that really stuck in my mind, that I almost found shocking at the time, was when he said that he believed that the Orthodox Churches had more in common with the great religions of the east, of Islam, Hinduism and Buddhism than with Western Christianity.

'You see, 'he said, 'just as they do, we believe that the purpose of life is to be found beyond death. The Western Church has sold out to the sociologists.'

Since then I have seen evidence of what he said about the Western Church. But that's not the whole picture. I am a Western Christian and I have been supported by that same Western Church in the belief that this life exists within the context of eternity.

waitangi day a family experience

More than twenty years ago now, I went with my children to an inculturalisation weekend at the Rehua Marae in Christchurch. The idea was to help Pakeha like us understand something of Maori custom and etiquette. Well, I think that was the idea and I suppose I imagined that we would be taught good manners for the Marae or something like that. I certainly wanted to know, partly because I am interested in different people's customs and attitudes but more particularly because I am a New Zealander.

The weekend was not as I'd imagined. I thought there would be a talk and that I would make notes, and maybe there would be group discussion and a bit of role-play to make it all clear, and of course there would be some activities for the children. It wasn't like that at all.

I remember once asking a Japanese friend how low to bow

when I met someone. He said, very politely, 'That, I cannot teach you. That, you learn when you are a baby, tied to your mother's back, and she bows.' I suppose he was saying that it's either in you from when you are born or it isn't.

The same difficulty for outsiders exists in Thai culture about how high you should hold your hands when you 'wai' someone. A 'wai' is putting the palms of your hands together in front of your face when you greet someone, so that you look rather as if you are saying your prayers. In Thailand, to greet a waiter in a restaurant in the same way that you greet a business man is to embarrass the first and show disrespect to the second. You can't win, or not at least until you have learned the system.

But that's Japan and Thailand and I'm not Japanese or Thai. I'm a New Zealander and that's the reason I went to the Rehua Marae in the first place.

By late on the Saturday afternoon I was feeling frustrated beyond measure. We were getting nowhere. It seemed to me that everything I did was wrong. If I tried and got the protocol wrong, I was wrong and if I didn't try I was wrong. It appeared that I couldn't be told 'how'. I was just supposed to 'know'. I should have been like the Japanese baby but it was too late. It all seemed to be an exercise in futility.

Then I realised that people were standing up in turn, singing a song, then speaking. So that was the way of it! I stood up, sang a short hymn, rather badly I suspect but that didn't seem to matter, and then I said what I thought. I pointed out that whatever I did I was in a 'no win' situation. If I didn't move in my understanding of Maori I was doing the wrong thing, and that if I did move, I'd get my feet cut off because I'd be sure to be wrong. Then I sat down. I suppose I felt better. I'd got it off my chest. No-one commented and that was that.

After the evening meal, we were sitting around the table talking and a Maori, older than me, said, 'Your mother was Kitty Ormond wasn't she?'

'Yes,' I said.

'I used to play tennis with Kitty at Waipukarau. Good looking girls, those Ormond girls. Probably still fine looking women.'

'Do you remember Aunt Fanny?' Aunt Fanny was my great aunt, my mother's aunt.

'Oh yes,' I said. 'Aunt Fanny and that ruddy ear trumpet.' Aunt Fanny was very deaf. Everyone smiled in a friendly way. My tennis playing friend called over his wife.

'We're just talking about Aunt Fanny,' he said.

'Oh, Aunt Fanny and that ruddy ear trumpet,' she said and everyone really laughed.

Her husband explained the laughter. 'That's what Simon has just said. She was his Aunt Fanny too.'

And his wife turned on me and said, 'Well! How could you go on about all that stuff in there, before dinner? All that about getting everything wrong! What are you on about? We're part of the same family.'

And I, close to tears said, 'But what if I hadn't been. What if my mother hadn't been an Ormond. What then?'

She paused, and said quite simply, 'Oh, we'd have found a way.'

heading home on the 159 bus

In London the other day, I was on a 159 bus heading home to Kennington, south of the river. I'd got on near Marble Arch and by the time we reached Oxford Circus and turned down Regent Street towards Piccadilly Circus, the bus was fairly full. I had a seat but some were standing.

Half way down Regent Street an elderly man climbed on, clearly in a bad mood. There was no seat for him.

'There are too many people in this country,' he said loudly to no one in particular and to everyone in general.

An attractive young woman standing near me, smiled and said to him, 'You're quite right. Some should go and live in Wales. We have lots of space in Wales.'

This was obviously not the answer that he was expecting. He glared at her, harrumphed and turning to a young, black man said, 'You should go back to where you came from.'

'What – Brixton?' he answered, pleasantly. Now Brixton's

just down the road from me in Kennington and this wasn't at all what old grumps meant.

The old man made one or two more disagreeable comments. The general atmosphere remained pleasantly tolerant and the young woman answered him back, totally nicely. Then, the old boy decided he'd had enough and moved to get off the bus. As he passed the young woman he glared at her. 'You're just stupid.'

Turning to me she said, 'Isn't it wonderful to be called stupid by a fascist!'

BUS
TAXI

the news the sport and the weather

It doesn't matter what country I am in. If I turn on the television or the radio it is always to find that immediately after the news, comes the sport and then the weather report. This seems to be a universal pattern and furthermore the editorial policy for the news invariably seems to be very different from the editorial policy for sports or weather reports.

Invariably, 'news' means bad news or even, as far as the news editors are concerned, 'tragic' news. Over a holiday weekend for example, the news is never about the wonderful time thousands of people are having but is more likely to be about the death toll on the roads. And it is bigger news if the death toll is greater than the year before. There may be other holiday news. Someone's campervan may have been burgled or a camp site may have been washed out. That is 'news'.

If that same editorial policy were applied to reporting sport, we would only hear of people sent off, of injuries or of matches abandoned because of the weather. We would hear of losses and failures but never the wins except perhaps a win by Australia which no doubt would count as bad news. The reality is that sports editors do give us the good news which they report enthusiastically.

There's an apparent shift though, in the editorial policy for weather reports. The presenters have learned their lesson. No more do their reports focus on those 'wonderfully hot, sunny, dry days ahead' when what is 'wonderful' for some may mean the continuation of terrible drought for others, and when the rain that is good news for the farmer may be bad news for the couple having a wedding in the garden. It seems that those presenting these reports have learned to restrict themselves to the facts and to leave opinion to the listener.

I tried out my theory of the three editorial policies on someone who was sitting next to me on a plane. He was an industrial psychologist involved in training senior management.

'You know, I think you're right,' he said and then added, 'I spend my time telling managers that the best way to motivate people and help them to get satisfaction out of their jobs is to give them positive feedback. Negative feedback does not help people learn and it leaves a department or company divided and less productive.' And he continued, 'Any teacher will tell you that continuing negative feedback to a pupil is simply destructive. I wonder what we're doing to our country when we only give negative news?'

Well, I didn't know either. But I did think how blissful it would be if the news editors went on a very long holiday and the editors of sport and weather reports took over.

the london bombings

After the London bombings we heard on radio's, 'What the papers say' of how the Spanish newspapers expressed amazement at the 'frigid' English and their calm reaction. The Spanish reaction to the Madrid bombings had been quite different. There were demonstrations in the streets and they brought the government down. The Spanish newspapers considered the British reaction to be 'unnatural and cold.'

I gather some New Zealand commentators referred to the British 'stiff upper lip' that in some way appeared to get people through the tragedy. I've always found that a rather silly expression and one not remotely appropriate in this case. 'Stiff upper lip' implies a lack of emotion. It implies distance and suggests a denial of an awful reality.

In London, there was emotion all right. People cried, at the time and after. They prayed and they called for help. Then, as one survivor described it, they sat in darkness, smoke and dirt trying to keep each other calm and, with characteristic London humour, even began telling jokes. A woman who had been trapped for twenty minutes amongst the debris of her underground carriage, told how a man called Ollie had said that he was used to dirt because he was a carpenter. Immediately, he was asked by someone else if he would come and fit some shelves in his front room. An actress said that she wasn't used to getting up so early and wondered if the tube was always like this at nine-twenty in the morning.

By the time their rescuers arrived, they all knew each other by name. Afterwards, one survivor said, 'Through the dirt-mist I could see the light of a torch and the orange jacket of an Underground worker. Slowly and incredibly calmly we began to move.' Even then, a man while getting out said he'd better leave his newspaper for someone else to read.

The following Monday one of those survivors used the Underground again. 'I was more nervous than I had expected,' she said, 'but I had to get to the job I'd been going to on Thursday'.

I don't think that that is 'stiff upper lip'. I just think it's one person's way of coping.

When the Queen made an informal visit to a hospital the day after the bombings she made a short speech. There was a catch in her voice. Emotion was very near the surface. Sebastian Coe who had just come back from the triumph of London being allocated the 2012 Olympics, was interviewed about the bombings. He cried.

I remember years ago having to tell someone that her adored younger brother had died. He was in his early forties and had survived the war and a prisoner of war camp. Suddenly, he had a heart attack and died, leaving a young family. His sister quite calmly thanked me for telling her and then said,

‘I think I’ll just go for a walk.’ I asked if she would like me to go with her and she said, ‘No thank you,’ and off she went.

There are different ways of coping with sadness and disaster. I haven’t come across anyone denying the reality of the awful things that happened in London on July 7. And I’ve rarely come across denial in other situations of personal tragedy. What I have learned is to allow people to cope in different ways and not to force my particular way on the Spanish, the English or indeed on anyone.

the new uniforms

I've just been on a long flight. Among the various announcements - pleased to have you on board, dinner soon, we hope you're going to enjoy this flight - was one I hadn't heard for a while. 'Some of our cabin crew are wearing the new, specially designed uniform. We do hope you like it and we would appreciate your comments.' Well I did like it. I liked the old uniform as well. As far as I was concerned, they both looked very smart indeed and I didn't feel any need to comment. Having seen the crew walking through the airport with their military looking caps, their braid and their immaculate white shirts, I was sure that all that smartness greatly contributed towards my feeling more confident about the flight in general. The whole thing clearly said that the nuts and bolts of the aeroplane, the electrical systems and all the rest must be OK if the staff looked so smart.

There has been quite a correspondence in newspapers in the United Kingdom about what professionals are expected to wear. It all started during the summer heat with lawyers not wanting to wear jackets and some doctors not keen to wear ties, now said to be unhygienic. Other doctors objected to a dress code for ward rounds. It seemed that casual clothing was more practical, more comfortable and perhaps made them seem more approachable. However, I gather that some patients - possibly older - have objected to young doctors with bare midriffs and pierced, tummy buttons. Nevertheless, dressing down seems to be the fashion.

I remember an old friend who some years ago was in a hospital in Christchurch. The consultant did his ward round with students in tow. He came to her bed and in the customary way asked her permission to continue his teaching round with the students while he examined her. I'm pretty sure he didn't expect any reaction other than a vague nod or a murmur of assent. That, however, was not the character of my elderly friend. 'Just one moment,' she said. The consultant and the students stopped, a little surprised. Then my friend turned to a student near her, looked him up and down, and asked, 'Young man. Are you untidy or do you choose to dress casually?'

The student, horrified at being the centre of attention, blushed and stammered out, 'I suppose I choose to dress casually.'

'Then I suppose I will put up with you. Because if I thought you were untidy in your dress I would know that you would be untidy in what you do as a doctor and then I wouldn't have you near me.' Turning back to the consultant she said, 'Continue.' And he did.

Later, the consultant came back to see her, thanked her for her comments and began to bemoan the casual attitudes of the young. At this point, she told him that the attitudes of the young were often formed by their elders and that it was he who should be making sure the students were tidy and not leaving it to her.

When I'm in New Zealand, I sometimes go to a local physiotherapist. I've a bad back and have been going to physios for years. This one goes bare foot. He wears baggy shorts, a singlet and a baseball cap back to front. To say he's casually dressed would be the understatement of the year. And, do you know, he is the best physio I've been to in my life!

discovering india discovering myself

It was New Year's Eve, 1965 when I arrived for the first time in India. I was twenty four years old – that was younger then than it is now – and this was to be my first experience, not just of India but of foreignness. I'd been in Europe before but had not met that extraordinary contrast – of people, of sight, of sound and colour, of smell, of air temperature, that is India.

We landed at Calcutta's Dum Dum airport. The atmosphere was hot and heavy. I went through immigration and customs and then there was a man holding up a card with my name on it. In those days the airline provided a car and a hotel if you didn't have an onward flight the same day. As I was going on to Katmandu two days later with no flights out until then, I was there at the airline's expense.

From the car, everything was a tired blur. We drove and drove and I made little sense of what I could see from the windows. The driver was pleasant though not particularly chatty. I was excited and a little nervous. Eventually, the car drew up outside the Great Eastern Hotel.

The hotel doorman came forward to open the car door, the driver got out to open the boot, a porter rushed to collect the suitcases and a man collapsed slowly and quietly onto the pavement between the car and the entrance to the hotel. He lay quite still. We walked around the body to get into the hotel.

One of the assistant managers, the one on night duty, came forward to welcome me.

'Could you do something,' I said. 'There's a man outside who has collapsed. I think he is very ill. He may be dying. He is just outside the hotel.'

'I do apologise, Sir,' said the night manager. 'I assure you, the body will be removed by the morning.' He thought I was making a complaint.

I'd encountered poverty before and walked past it but I don't think I had really seen it until India.

In 1984, I deliberately returned to Bombay, now called Mumbai, to see the poverty, and as I thought, to be confronted by its reality and sort out my understanding of it. How simplistic and how arrogant. I was old enough to know better.

The plane arrived in the middle of the night. It seems always to be so for planes coming in from Australia or New Zealand. And that time of night, two or three in the morning, has a particular atmosphere. It is the time when the heart beats slowest, when we sleep most peacefully and when we die most easily. This time there was no one to meet me. I took a taxi.

For some reason, I don't know why, as we drove from the airport to the hotel, I decided to count the number of people I saw sleeping on the road. And I mean asleep in the street, not on the pavement, not in makeshift shelters, not in concrete sewer pipes waiting to be laid, but sleeping in the street which really meant the gutter. Within a few minutes of leaving the airport perimeter, I had counted over a hundred people and I gave up.

The poverty of Bombay was loathsome and I couldn't deal with it at all. The wonderfully grand, Indian Victorian Gothic architecture, the Elephanta Caves: I could stand none of it. I left Bombay earlier than planned for the known realities of Europe, something I had never done before and have not done since. Now, I always find that there is something positive to respond to in a place. But not so then. Not for me. Not Bombay. Not India.

On my next visit to that country, I met a woman, a beggar who lived in the bus shelter that I used every day when I went into the centre of New Delhi.

She was always there. The bus shelter protected her to some extent from rain or sun. She owned, from what I could tell, two bricks. They appeared to be very important. She needed them to stand on when the rains poured their water across the pavement. This way she could keep her feet and the bottom of her sari dry. And she had a bag, though I don't know what was in it. But she also had a smile, a sense of humour and a personality such that even though we didn't share a language, a background or anything other than our humanity, we began to get to know each other. I started to realise then, that it was only when I stopped seeing her as one of 'the poor' and saw her as herself, that there was hope – hope for me, that is. And then I understood how that applied to anyone – 'rich', 'poor', 'black', 'white', 'conservative', 'radical'. As long as I saw only the category, the label, I was lost. If I really saw the person, then there was hope, hope of coming to know others and in time of coming to love India.

Then I was in India in 1995, arriving inevitably in the middle of the night at New Delhi's Indra Ghandi International Airport. India seemed in the midst of a party. This time, driving into town I could see whole families, dressed up to the nines, on their way home, laughing and celebrating. It was Dusshera, the Hindu festival of hope, celebrating the triumph of good over evil.

I was in Jaipur for the culmination of the festival when, the Mayor having made a speech to the crowds, someone dressed as the Lord Rama and looking remarkably like St George setting out to slay the dragon, mounted a white horse and rode across the padang. He shot a flaming arrow at the effigy of the demon king. The gigantic effigy burst into flame and fireworks and everyone cheered.

The next day, I sent a fax to a friend in New Zealand. It read, 'Last night the Lord Rama most satisfactorily destroyed the Demon King at the fairground in Jaipur. I was there along with some 3000 others. There is hope. Good was seen to overcome evil.'

the traffic lights

I heard of an elderly woman in Australia living, I think, in a Melbourne suburb. She was going to dinner with her son and daughter in law and driving herself. When she came to a set of traffic lights, she stopped. They were on red.

Two hours after she was due to arrive for dinner, her son became worried and phoned her home because he thought she must have been delayed. There was no answer. He phoned the police. The police shortly found her waiting in her car at the red traffic light. The lights were faulty. They were stuck on red. She was asked why she hadn't driven carefully forward through the lights.

'I couldn't, they were on red. You have to obey the law.'

The other day I was in Bangkok, at a friend's house. Two more people arrived. One of them, a Canadian who speaks Thai fluently was laughing when he arrived, so I asked what was funny.

At the end of the street there were traffic lights. His Thai friend who was driving, went through the red light and was pulled over by a policeman.

'You drove through a red light,' said the policeman.

'Yes, I did.'

'Didn't you see the red light?'

'Oh yes, I saw the red light,' said the driver, 'but I didn't see you.'

The policeman was so delighted with the honesty of the reply, or possibly the cheek of it, that he let him off.

Now here's a law abider and a law breaker. This time it was the law breaker who came out of it best.

And for me it brings to mind a totally different issue. In London at the moment, there are all sorts of new regulations and by-laws but there doesn't seem to be anyone round to enforce them. It's as if the authorities are assuming that we are a law abiding nation rather than law breakers. They think that all you need to do is to bring in a bit of new legislation and everyone will fall into line. They take for granted that people will obey the law simply because it is the law and that we'll all stop at red lights. I'm afraid they're making a mistake.

More and more, people are just going ahead hoping there's not a policeman round the corner.

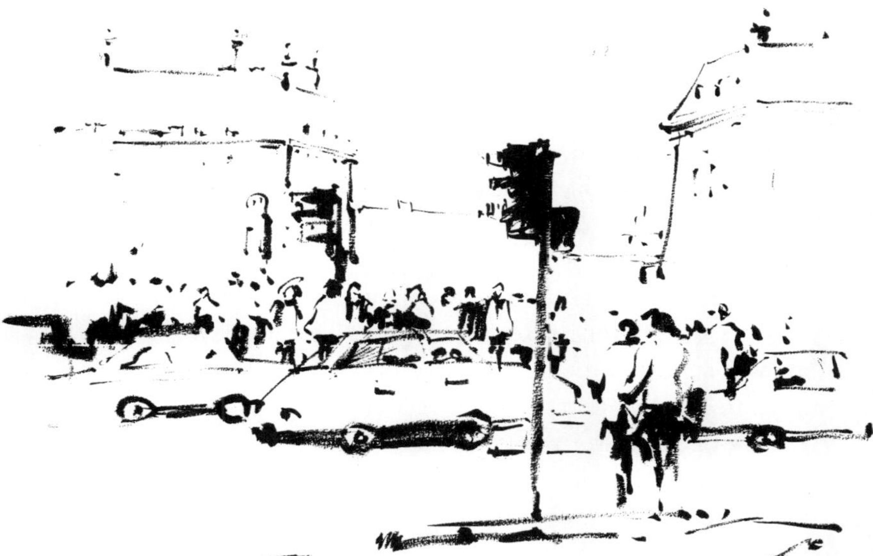

easter

facing reality alone

There is something awful, something frightening about being abandoned, feeling deserted. But deserting a friend and having to go on living with yourself would surely be worse? In both cases there is simply the reality of yourself and your own resources.

Odette Hallowes, known to many as Odette Churchill, fought for the French Resistance in the Second World War. She was captured, held in Fresnes prison near Paris and later taken to Ravensbruck Concentration Camp.

She spoke afterwards about what it was like to be in solitary confinement. For her, being alone was more painful than the torture she underwent but never gave into. Her fellow resistance fighters were never betrayed but she found the loneliness of captivity almost unendurable.

Then one day in the autumn of 1942 a leaf floated through the window of her cell. That leaf became for her a symbol of life, of continuity and the cycle of nature. That leaf enabled her to endure solitary confinement because she knew, through its veins, its shape, and its colour, that even as it had fallen, others would come to life in the spring. Odette knew that she was part of something much greater than her captivity or her captors, that ultimately she was not alone and that life would continue. .

Vaclav Havel, President of the Czech Republic, was put into solitary confinement by the Communists. He thought the loneliness would drive him mad. Then he was given a letter, a censored letter. In a cruel joke, his captors had blacked out the entire contents. He did not even know who it was from. But the letter was in an envelope and on the envelope there was a stamp. The letter had come from England and on the stamp was the Queen's head. For Havel, that stamp became an icon, a means whereby he could see through to a greater truth and a greater reality than his cell. He was able to think of a person and a free nation and a whole way of life of which because of a postage stamp, he was a part. That stamp saved his sanity.

I think a lot of that is what Good Friday is all about. It's about facing reality alone, being deserted by friends as Jesus was. It's about being held captive or living a solitary existence in a flat with no one coming to visit, or being alone in a crowd. Good Friday is about facing our own realities with our own resources. But in the facing of these realities, along with Odette or Havel, we may pick up our own leaf or postage stamp, respond to them and find life again. The leaves are there for all of us but the response has to be ours. Or like Jesus' disciples, the deserters, we can face the cross and respond to God's forgiveness and love.

a time
to endure

When you travel by air there's a time you have to spend in airports after you've checked in and before your flight is called that is a sort of limbo. I know that if you are well organised you have a book and you read it but it's still not a very settled time. International flights are worse because you have gone through customs and passport control. You can't go back and you can't go forward. You are in a 'no man's land'.

Apparently, even in airports where 'duty free' has been abolished, the shops still do a roaring trade. This is because we don't know what to do with this sort of non time and so we shop. Shopping is familiar and comforting. It fills in the time but it doesn't achieve anything and you simply end up with a lot of stuff you neither need nor want.

One of the really difficult times in life is the time between the death of someone we love and the funeral. There is the planning for the funeral of course but when that's been done, even though there are people coming and going to say how sorry they are and bringing a plate of something or a casserole just in case – there's still the emptiness, the compulsory pause, the trying to come to terms with it all. They say that we are in a state of shock.

I have always found Holy Saturday to be like that. It is an in between day. The day between the crucifixion and the resurrection. There are no particular services and the day is just one of hanging around, waiting.

So what is this day for? I think it's a time to face the

limbo that exists for all of us, sometime. And the best thing to do with it is just to bear it, knowing that sometimes there just is nothing to do other than to bear it - to endure. No more. No less.

the light of christ

I was in Greece for Easter a few years ago now. It was Orthodox Easter which is later than ours. They work to a different calendar. I was in Athens and late at night on Easter Eve I decided to go to the little hilltop church of St George above Kolonaki.

A lot of Athenians had made the same choice so the church and the square outside were packed. St George's on the sharply pointed hill of Likavittos seemed to be making a small Christian gesture at the ancient pagan Parthenon on the Acropolis across the city. And on that Easter Eve the son et lumiere which nightly lights up the Acropolis was switched off leaving Athens dark and still.

The blackness of the night, the stars, the stillness and the ancient chants of the priests, the gold vestments all combine to create the mystical atmosphere. And then the climax of the service. The priest comes before the people holding high three lighted candles bound together, the light of the resurrection. And he calls out the ancient chant, 'Christos aneste!' Christ is risen!

And this becomes the Easter greeting as people say to one another, 'Christos aneste!

And others reply, 'Alethos aneste!' He is risen indeed!

From the priest's candles, the people light their candles and those further away light theirs from those closer in, one from another, all greeting each other in the same way. Quite soon, the service is finished – except that it's not finished.

People pour out of the packed church smiling, greeting one another, holding their lighted candles. And they set off home down the winding steps from the hilltop church.

That year I stayed outside the church and looked out over the city. I saw the river of light - candlelight, pouring down the sides of the hill. And then the river becoming little streams, then trickles of light, then pin points of light in the distance.

And I knew that each light was being taken into someone's home – a flat, a room, a house. And that there, the lamp in front of the icon, the holy picture that has a place in every Greek home, the lamp that had been put out since Good Friday - that lamp was lit from the Easter Resurrection light.

The light of the Risen Christ had found its place and shone in every dwelling.

you can pray

It was on a BBC TV programme – 'Any Questions', I think, broadcast on Thursday evenings in the UK and usually hosted by one of the Dimblebys. It's certainly one of the more intellectual programmes in terms of who it is aimed at, and there's a live audience, fairly switched on politically and intellectually. The audience put the questions to the panel. I'm sure that the whole thing is planned and vetted before it goes on air and certainly they make sure that the panel members cover a different range of views.

The subject was one of the natural disasters the world had faced during 2005. I think it was the famine in Dafur and the panel were being asked about different ways of dealing with it. Comparisons were being made with the recent Tsunami and how people had reacted to that. Then one of the audience asked the question, 'But what can we do? I feel so helpless in the face of these distant disasters. What can I do?'

Various members of the panel tried to answer the question. They floundered. One of the panellists, Liberal Democrat Member of Parliament, Simon Hughes, tried to answer and finished with, 'But of course you can pray.'

The audience laughed.

On the 7th of July last year we had the bombings on the London Underground and the London Transport bus. Reporters interviewed some of those involved. One person said that people were really afraid; many were crying, others were praying.

A woman spoke of holding the hand of someone who had been very badly injured and was dying. She told of how she had done her best to calm and comfort her. 'I just held her hand and said the Lord's Prayer, quietly. Then I said it again.'

Of course on Television's Question Time, the audience's laughter as a reaction to Simon Hughes', 'You can pray' was because it was just that: a television show.

The London Underground bombings were a reality, and people prayed.

the children of angkor

At the entrance to every one of the great ruined temples and monuments of Cambodia's Angkor, there is a group of children with things to sell. These children are not beggars. They are salesmen, budding entrepreneurs. The magnificent monuments of Angkor are spread over an area of seventy square miles and there are more than twenty major sites, not archaeological digs but the ruins of towering temples and palaces with moats and lakes set in the jungle. There are good sealed roads between the monuments, so you can go by car or if you are brave and built that way, you can get there on the pillion of a motorbike.

Arriving at a particular ruin, you show an attendant your Angkor pass, a laminated card with your name and photo. Instantly, you are surrounded by young salesmen aged from about seven to twelve. They're not skipping school. In Cambodia, schools have two sessions, morning and afternoon, so at midday it's change over time and there's a fair chance that many of these young salesmen are using the money they make to pay their modest school fees.

But however delightful the children and however worthy the cause, there is a limit to the number of bamboo whistles and t-shirts, tablecloths and guide books that the traveller can carry, use or need. And there's another thing about children. They may be delightful but they're noisy. They call to one another at the tops of their voices, sing and shout. It's their nature. Mostly I like to visit temples quietly. The peace of the place and the noises of the jungle are what I enjoy.

So, I had an idea. At each monument I selected one child, usually the one I thought would make a good teacher when she grew up – one with a bit of authority - and then I'd negotiate a price for her to keep the others quiet when they were near me. That system worked really well.

At some monuments I wanted a guide and at others I didn't. At Angkor Wat I didn't but a small boy insisted, saying, 'But have you seen the North Gate?'

I admitted I hadn't and he said I must and that he'd show me. It was quite a walk and my curiosity was aroused when my small guide said in a rather conspiratorial way,

'I like going to the north gate.'

'Why?'

'Because I like to see the cow boys.'

'Cowboys?' I thought, 'In Cambodia? At Angkor?' Stetsons and spurs did seem a bit out of place. Then as we were walking on a wide mown swathe cut through the jungle, I heard this voice full of joy saying, 'Look! look! There are the cowboys.' And sure enough, nearer the jungle there were water buffalo with their young herdsmen who had taken the animals to graze. My guide called and waved to the cowboys and the cowboys called and waved back.

But my most important experience with the children of Angkor was at the entrance to Bantei Srei the 'citadel of the women'. This time as I was going in, knowing that I did want to buy some t- shirts for presents, I said to the surrounding children, 'Not now. Later, when I come out.' And they left me alone. They are very good like that. They don't carry on pestering the visitors. When I did come out, I bought some bits and pieces and a t-shirt from the children who crowded round me. Then, just as I was leaving, a small boy of about eight confronted me. He looked straight at me, reproachfully and his voice quavering and with tears welling in his eyes, he said, 'When you went in you said you would buy a T-shirt from me.' And, having made the accusation, he turned and walked away. He was right. I had. I'd forgotten and so had not kept my word. I called after him, 'I'm sorry. I do want to buy a t-shirt from you.'

He said, 'Buy two!' And I did.

Some would say he was just a good salesman. I say that he was just a small boy who expected adults to keep their word. And he was a good salesman.

a visit to the doctor

I went to see the doctor. I don't go often and I'm certainly not a hypochondriac but there were one or two problems that were bothering me.

Well, I've had a bad back for years and it was playing up. Then there was my right shoulder. That wasn't too good either. Generally I was fine but there were things I was finding quite difficult to do so I knew there was something wrong.

I'd been to that doctor before. I knew she was excellent. She was one of the team at the local medical centre. She asked a lot of questions, I was made to stand up and sit down, then get up again and move around. It all seemed very thorough. She is a very capable doctor. At the end of it all she said, 'Well, Mr Acland, I'm afraid we're going to have to put it down to the ageing process.' The 'ageing process'! I had never been told anything so ridiculous before. There had to be a pill or some medicine that would fix things. Perhaps an X-ray would reveal a straightforward problem and then I would rapidly and painlessly be cured. Not a bit of it. It was being put down to the ageing process!

My doctor did not give me a prescription, nor did she refer me to a specialist. She did, however, suggest some things I should be doing. A proper exercise regime for a start and then, 'If you do the exercises and are not better in six weeks you should come and see me again.' So, I did the exercises and after six weeks I was a great deal better. I was also more than a little put out. The ageing process indeed.

Then an old friend who had a bad knee went to her doctor. After an examination he said to her, 'I'm afraid there's not much we can do. We're just going to have to put it down to the ageing process.'

'I don't think so,' replied my friend. 'You see, Doctor, this knee is bad but I have another knee and it's perfectly fine. And the interesting thing is that both my knees are the same age. Let's look at it again shall we?'

and how old was she?

It was at a dinner in Bangkok and we were eating in an Italian restaurant. There must have been about eight or ten of us and I was the only New Zealander. There was an English couple but most of the others, including our host who was the only one I knew, were Americans. Sitting on my right was an American woman who was both interesting and fun. Well on into the meal she asked me, 'How old do you think I am?'

Now, that's an awkward question in any language and especially so in my experience if it is asked by a woman. She was waiting for an answer and I thought quickly. She was probably about 55, but I knew that it is never a good idea to be too accurate in the matter of age. I went for the previous decade. 'I think you are 49.'

She smiled, 'Simon, I'm seventy.'

It was quite obvious that she wasn't and I said so.

'Ask,' she said, indicating our host. So I asked him.

'Oh, she's at least seventy!'

Along with everyone else, the woman laughed and said, 'I've had surgery. I've had everything done. And when I say, everything I mean everything.'

Now, I don't know anything about plastic surgery and I thought it best not to enquire too deeply into the 'everything' but simply to say what I believed to be true.

'Well, you look wonderful.'

The dinner continued and at one stage I said that I thought it ridiculous that here we all were in Bangkok but we were eating at an Italian restaurant. 'Why don't we get together at a very good Thai restaurant?' Everyone seemed to think it a good idea and my new friend said she would call me to confirm the arrangement.

A couple of days later, I was in my hotel room and the phone rang. I answered it and someone began talking to me. The voice was female, elderly and American but I couldn't think who it was. I listened carefully, wracking my brains to put a face to the voice. Then the penny dropped. It was my friend from the other evening. She was unrecognisable. The 'everything' she had had done had not included her voice. I still found her entertaining and interesting but the sound of the voice that was speaking to me was that of the seventy year old that she actually was.

burma or myanmar

I had wanted to visit Burma for years. One of my uncles who trained as a singer had 'The Road to Mandalay' as part of his repertoire. As a child, I used to sit on the floor of my grandmother's sitting room listening to an old gramophone record of him singing of flying fish and pagodas, of temple bells and the dawn coming up like thunder out of China "cross the bay' and I'd imagine this strange, distant, exotic place.

But I couldn't go to Burma because from 1962 it was virtually closed to the outside world. The Burmese government rejected colonialism and western imperialism, barred its doors and decided to go its own way.

Now you can get a tourist visa without any difficulty but first of all you will have to make a moral decision as to whether or not you should be going there at all. And you have to decide whether to call the country 'Burma' or 'Myanmar' and that can be seen as part of the same problem.

It's all to do with what we think is the right way to deal with those countries whose regimes are not just different from ours but are oppressive. It's part of the same argument and concern that so many of us had over South Africa when apartheid ruled. To go or not to go? The same moral question applies now, I suppose, to going to Tibet or Zimbabwe.

Burma is ruled by a military dictatorship which was called the 'State Law and Order Restoration Council' –' SLORC'. It soon gained a reputation to match the sound of its name - one repressive of human rights, opposed to freely elected, democratic government and holding ruthlessly to its control over the Burmese people. In 1997 it changed its name to the 'State Peace and Development Council', slightly cleaned up its act but basically continued on its former oppressive ways.

This is where the problem of whether to call the country 'Burma' or 'Myanmar' comes in. It was the military rulers who introduced the name change from the English - 'Union of Burma' to the indigenous - 'Union of Myanmar'. So whose side are you on if you call it 'Myanmar'?

The British get around it by calling the country 'Myanmar' and then 'Burma' in brackets. I'm inclined to wander back and forth between the two.

Today, the voice of the opposition is its leader Aung San Suu Kyi. Her father founded the Myanmar independence movement and was assassinated in 1947. Aung San Suu Kyi, often referred to as 'The Lady', certainly captures the imagination, managing somehow to carry the ideals of freedom while being kept under house arrest and continual harassment by the government.

Aung San Suu Kyi has said that tourists should not visit Myanmar because to do so would be to support the current oppressive regime. The locals must make the economic sacrifice that doing without tourism entails. But others within her own party, and the opposition in exile, say that to visit Myanmar/Burma is to support the people economically and psychologically. Only if people have food can they begin to oppose the oppressors. The moral argument goes back and forth.

One of the most popular travel guides, 'Lonely Planet', caused quite a stir when it published a guide to Myanmar. Was this supporting the government? Certainly it is the only guide book that I know of that has at its beginning a major article headed, 'Should you visit Myanmar?' But by the time you have read the article you have already bought the book and you are probably on your way.

I have listened to the arguments and I have thought about the issues. But if I'm honest, I went to Myanmar(Burma) because Uncle Mick sang 'The Road to Mandalay' and I wanted to go.

the laos under 16 football team

I flew into Yangon, Myanmar(Burma), from Bangkok 'Thai International'. It's a fairly standard flight like going from Auckland to Christchurch, though there is a one hour time change so you have to adjust your watch. I was sitting in my favourite seat, near the front and to the side.

The middle section of the plane was filled with a party of young men, obviously a team of some sort. We began to talk, in a fairly limited way because English is my only language. Anyway it turned out that they were members of the Laos Under Sixteen Football Team on their way to Yangon to play in a football tournament against teams from Myanmar, Malaysia, and Guam.

I explained that I was from New Zealand and one of them knew where New Zealand was and told the others. I was none too sure where Laos is. For the record, at its borders are Thailand, Myanmar, China, Vietnam, and Cambodia and it is entirely landlocked. The footballers were pleased to hear of New Zealand and asked me questions about it. I explained what I could and said that rugby was really our thing. Some of them seemed to know that already.

Before we landed, the air hostess came through the plane to give orchids to the women passengers. The footballers didn't realise that the orchids were only for the women - that discrimination is not their custom - and rather shocked, they asked the hostess why she hadn't given one to me. She of course gave me an orchid which I then presented to the captain of the Laos team as a sign of New Zealand-Laos friendship. Very pleased, he pinned it on his jersey. We were all rather pleased with ourselves and left the plane the best of friends.

In the terminal there was the usual business of immigration and customs and before I met my guide, I saw the Laos football team lined up to have their photo taken for the local paper. The captain pointed proudly to the orchid still pinned to his jersey. They smiled and waved to me and we wished each other well.

I took a taxi into town and checked in at my hotel. Having completed the formalities, I turned from the reception desk and who should I see coming through the door but the team from Laos. It was as if we were old friends who hadn't seen each other for years. The next morning, when I came down stairs, I realised that also staying in the hotel were the Malaysian and the Guam football teams, each having their breakfast in a different dining room. Needless to say, I had been placed with the Laos team.

As best we could, we discussed football strategy and the fact that they, and I for that matter, had a strong suspicion that some of the players in the other teams were over sixteen.

'He lost his birth certificate,' one of my friends said darkly as a very mature sixteen year old from the Malaysian Team walked past. There were also rumours about the age of members of the Myanmar Team but none of us had seen them as they were staying somewhere else.

Sadly, I had to leave Yangon before the tournament began and we all agreed that I should have organised things better. On the day I was leaving, the coach asked me if I would come to say goodbye to the team. He made a short speech thanking me for my encouragement and support, gave me a Laos football jersey and pinned on my shirt a sort of medal. 'You are now,' he said, 'a member of the Laos Under Sixteen Football Team'. Everyone clapped. I thanked them and thought, 'Not bad for an overweight fifty nine year old New Zealander who has never played football in his life.'

a face on the underground

I enjoy travelling on the tube. Well I like the double-decker buses too, but the underground has a particular atmosphere. This may be because there's nothing really to look at except the others in the carriage. Through the window there's only the tunnel wall. Some people read a book or a newspaper and I've even seen others marking exam papers or reading 'Strictly Confidential' documents. I usually have a look. So, I have noticed, does the person on the other side. Though I've not yet read anything especially exciting, I haven't given up.

In London, I live in Kennington on the Northern Line. One Sunday, about midday going north on the tube, I watched a woman putting on full make-up. From nothing, she progressed through several layers of powder carefully applied with brushes, lip colour, actually many colours, to false eyelashes, eye shadow - the lot. She achieved all this holding a tiny mirror in one hand and an open bag on her lap, meanwhile juggling small jars and flat packs that looked just like old-fashioned, watercolour paint boxes. Throughout all of this, the train continued its uneven way, swaying, stopping, starting again and lurching on.

She seemed to be going for a layered effect. Colour was applied then brushed off. Another colour went on, was smoothed in and again the brushing process began but this time stopped before all was removed. Sometimes the brush was exchanged for a little stick. Little dots of liquid colour were added. The whole carriage followed each step. We were riveted.

Between Kennington and Tottenham Court Road, just five stops, all was successfully completed. Admittedly, there was a delay between Waterloo and Embankment – something to do with temporary signal failure at Camden Town. That bought her valuable extra time, enough to put on the eyelashes. Now that really did seem an operation to be attempted only by the true professional. They came in a special box and appeared to have some sort of self stick adhesive. Once on, they were blackened using a small corkscrew like instrument she pulled out of a narrow tube. She tidied up her eyebrows and a stray hair was deftly removed. A very satisfactory conclusion to an expert performance.

When she had finished, we almost clapped. They say that travel broadens the mind. It is certainly amazing what you can learn travelling on the London Underground.

anzac day

My father was a Member of Parliament during much of the second world war and one of the duties my mother had was to be with the official party when they farewelled the troops before they left to serve overseas. It was also her duty in her role as president of the local Red Cross to visit families when they heard the news of the death of a son, a husband or a father. She was only in her early thirties, with four children under ten and she told me she felt totally inadequate. 'But,' she said, 'it was one of those things that had to be done. Someone had to do it, so why shouldn't it be me?'

Standing on the stage at one of those farewells, she heard the local Catholic priest, an old man, say quite simply, 'The sorrows of a mother's heart, no man can tell.'

She spoke too, of going to tell one local farming family of a young son and husband killed in action. His parents were sitting there in the kitchen. The young man's wife, his widow now, was feeding her baby. Another time she had to tell a widow that both her sons had been killed. That was part of my mother's being 'at war' while still at home.

I sat one night at a dinner party and we began to talk about that war. I realised as the meal progressed that of the eight of us, all of whom were my contemporaries in their late fifties or early sixties, five had never known their fathers. They had all been killed in action. One of the men, a Canadian, said that when he was 50, he had been at a conference in Norway and realising he was somewhere near to where his father was buried, the father he'd never known, he went to find his grave. When he found it, he looked at the gravestone. It was that of a 28 year old. He said he felt like a father looking at the gravestone of his son.

One of the women spoke with great affection of her stepfather and all who had had stepfathers said that they had really been loved by them. Then she said, 'My mother told me how she had met my father when he was on leave and how they fell in love. On his next leave they married. On the third I was conceived. There never was a fourth. He was killed in Burma.'

Another woman whose mother hadn't remarried had two brothers. They lived on little money and a lot of love. Yet another remembered screaming in terror when at the age of four a strange man had appeared at home, a gaunt, terrifying figure, and she was told he would be living with them. He had been in a prisoner of war camp. It was her first encounter with her father.

There are memorials for the men and women who died in war. We do remember them. That evening we remembered the women whose experience of war had been at home. Somehow they had survived. Many of them had triumphed.

the golden mystery of burma

"Then a golden mystery upheaved itself on the horizon, a beautiful, winking, wonder that blazed in the sun. A shape that was neither Muslim dome nor Hindu temple spire. 'There's the old Shwedagon', said my companion."

Thus, Rudyard Kipling wrote in 'Letters from the East' in 1898.

Today, Myanmar/Burma's Shwe Dagon Pagoda is still like that - absolute perfection. Its gold covered bell-shaped stupa rises skywards from its octagonal base for 98 metres to its diamond-encrusted tip. From the distance this golden spire seems to hover, to float above the jungle and it gives to Yangon and to all of Burma a sense of holiness.

When you come out from the covered walkway onto the great marble platform of the Shwe Dagon, you are dazzled by the intensity of light reflected not only from the central gold spire but from the smaller stupas, temples, statues, shrines and pavilions that surround it. All sparkle with life and beauty.

The Shwe Dagon Pagoda is a shrine, a great shrine on a hill, built to enclose some sacred hairs from the head of the Buddha. The story goes that the Buddha plucked from his own head eight strands of hair and gave them to two brothers, Burmese merchants who were travelling in India. When they were on their way back to Myanmar four of the sacred hairs were stolen. There were many other trials and tribulations for the brothers but with the help of the spirit world they arrived in Myanmar with the remaining four sacred hairs and there was a great festival.

Then the Lord of Heaven came down to earth to help choose the site for the shrine and a vault was dug. When the casket containing the hairs was opened, instead of four hairs the original 8 hairs flew up, 'to the height of seven palm trees, emitting rays of variegated hues with such a dazzle that the dumb could speak, the deaf could hear, the lame could walk and a rain of jewels fell knee deep'. The hairs returned to the casket and it was buried. A gold slab was placed on top of the vault and a pagoda was built, first brick, then iron, then marble, lead, copper, tin, silver and the whole thing covered in gold. That is the legend and it has it that all this happened about 2500 years ago.

Archaeologists date the present stupa to between the 6th and 10th centuries. Whatever we believe of the history, myth and legend surrounding the Shwe Dagon Pagoda, it is the most sacred place in all Myanmar for Burmese Buddhists. It is their place of pilgrimage and is quite wonderful.

All this built for ancient legend and for eight hairs from the head of a good teacher. It may seem rather strange to us but there is, I think, something universal here.

St Peter's in Rome is built over the tomb, the very bones,

of the holy apostle St Peter. And many churches throughout Christendom have within them, relics of the saints and martyrs. Only the other day, I went to a service in London's Westminster Abbey. At the end of the service there was a procession to the shrine of St Edward the Confessor. In the shrine are his bones.

I suspect many Westerners find holy places easier to deal with than personal relics. We seem to be uncomfortable in our western sophistication, with the idea, let alone the reality, of keeping and honouring parts of the bodies of those we have loved.

And yet having said that, many of us know that funerary lockets and brooches containing a lock of hair of a beloved departed were worn by our Victorian great grandmothers. For some of us, the ashes of those who have been cremated are not simply scattered to the wind or buried but are kept in an urn in a special place in the house. And how many families have kept one of those baby teeth for which the fairies brought sixpence or fifty cents? And then there's the baby's footprint taken soon after birth and now treasured, in the Baby Book.

Perhaps photos have become the twenty first century's relics. Displayed on mantelpiece or bookcase or more reverently preserved in photo albums, these likenesses rather than more tangible parts of the person have become the symbols of our honoured remembrance.

But whatever our shrines may be today, if we remember our honoured dead with anything even a fraction as moving and beautiful as the Shwe Dagon Pagoda, how blest we will be.

the olive counter at harrods

Christchurch has Ballantynes, Wellington has Kirkaldies, Auckland has Smith and Caughey and London has Harrods. But Harrods has what none of the others has. It has a food hall. Well, not even a food hall but a series of food halls. Vast, pillared, decorated spaces for every food you can think of.

There's the fish department where a fountain displays the catch of the day against a background of mermaids. One department leads to another – meat, a bakery, a patisserie and through to exotic fruits from around the world, pates and puddings, sushi and sausages – and olives.

I had been told there were some very good olives in a herb dressing at Harrods and as I was passing anyway, I went in. There was a queue at the olive counter but I had time so I joined it. When it was my turn, I said hello to the young West Indian behind the counter and told him what I wanted.

He half turned to get my olives then turned back to me and said, 'Do you hate anyone?'

I was a bit surprised but I thought for a moment and replied, 'No. I don't believe I do.'

He gave the deepest sigh and said, 'How do you manage it. I really don't want to hate anyone.'

Well, then I really had to think and I told him that I thought the reason I didn't hate anyone is because basically I'm fairly lazy. 'I think hate takes a lot of energy,' I said.

And I told him that I probably had hated different people at different times, at least for a few minutes but that I didn't have the stamina for sustained hatred. I also said something about seeing the other person more as a person rather than focusing on the particular thing they'd done that had made me hate them.

Then I turned to the English woman behind me in the queue and asked her what she thought. I knew that she couldn't have helped but hear our conversation. She'd never thought about it much but added that whenever she 'wasn't speaking' to someone she always forgot that she wasn't speaking to them, and spoke. So it rather ruined the effect.

'Any help?' I said to the young man.

'Maybe,' he said doubtfully and then added, 'But you see there are some people I just can't abide.'

'Oh, there are lots of people I can't abide,' I said, 'but I don't hate them.'

And from about five back in the queue a voice said, 'I am finding this really interesting but if I don't get home soon with my olives my husband's really going to hate me.' So I took my olives and left.

number one london

Number One, London. That is a grand address! And Apsley House is a very grand house. It has Hyde Park at its back and at its front is one of the busiest roundabouts in central London. But it wasn't always like this. Originally, the house was the first in a row of similar grand houses that went from Hyde Park Corner along towards Piccadilly. Had you lived in the eighteenth century, it was the first house that you would have come to after passing the toll gates at the top of Knightsbridge.

Once the home of the first Duke of Wellington, the Iron Duke, the house along with its contents was given to the nation in 1947. It is recognised as being one of the best, small museums in London.

The grandest room in the house is the Waterloo Gallery. It is of course named after the Battle of Waterloo when, in 1815, the Iron Duke finally beat Napoleon. The Gallery, designed by Benjamin Dean Wyatt, was added to the original house especially to display the Duke's magnificent collection of paintings. Many of them were presented to the Duke by King Ferdinand VII of Spain in gratitude for being rid of the Bonapartes.

The windows of the Waterloo gallery are fitted with sliding mirrors so that in the evening they reflect the lights of the two, great, floor standing chandeliers given to the Duke by the emperor, Nicholas the first of Russia. When the gallery is used as a dining room the table which can seat eighty five people is assembled around these chandeliers. This table is so wide that you can barely see the person opposite you because down the centre of the table is a fairly extraordinary table decoration. It is the twenty six foot long centrepiece of what is known as the Portuguese Service, given in gratitude by the Portuguese for deliverance from Napoleon. The central ornament of the whole thing, made of silver and gold, shows the four continents paying tribute to the armies of Britain, Portugal and Spain. It is neo-classical and there are dancing figures, once linked by garlands of silk flowers. It is serious stuff.

The house and its contents are impressive but it is the man himself, the first Duke of Wellington who is really fascinating. He was born Arthur Wellesley in 1769, in Dublin. Once asked, whether being born in Dublin didn't make him Irish, he replied, 'If you're born in a stable it doesn't make you a horse.'

Wellesley's father died when he was twelve and when the boy was seventeen his mother remarked that her 'ugly boy, Arthur' was only 'fit for powder' – gunpowder, so he was sent to a military academy in France for a year and ended up in the British army.

Adored by his men, Wellesley was one of those leaders who would not eat before the men had eaten or sleep before he knew they had somewhere to rest. He was the soldier who said, 'Next to a battle lost, the greatest misery is a battle gained.' His defeat of Napoleon at Waterloo was the culmination of his military career.

But the Duke, created Marques of Douro and Duke of Wellington in 1814, was also a statesman. He served in India both as soldier and administrator and after Waterloo in 1818, he re-entered politics. By 1828, he was Prime Minister. He was not a comfortable politician nor always a popular one. The windows of Apsley house were more than once broken by a stone throwing mob so that the 'Iron Duke' had iron shutters fitted. Serving as Foreign Secretary in the government of Sir Robert Peel and with Peel in opposition, he said of himself and Peel,

'I have no small talk and Peel has no manners.'

A long lasting marriage did not prevent his being a great womaniser. His close friend, Mrs Arbuthnot, influenced much of the decoration of Apsley House. But impervious to scandal and in reply to a blackmail threat, it was he who said, 'Publish and be damned.'

Amongst the many paintings, hanging low down where it has always hung in the Waterloo Gallery, there is a small painting by Corregio. It was the Iron Duke's favourite painting. Unusually for an oil painting, it is covered with glass. Or rather it is in a locked, glass fronted frame. The key to the lock was always on the Duke's watch chain. He would open the case, dust the painting with a silk handkerchief and gaze and gaze at it.

And the subject of the favourite painting of this soldier, womaniser, statesman? Jesus in agony in the garden of Gethsemane the night before the crucifixion.

funny my works

Whenever I travel, and it's a Sunday, I try to find a Christian Church where I can go to communion. Afterwards, I choose a holy place of the country I'm in, and go there just to be quiet for a while. In Bangkok, I usually go to Wat Phra Chetuphon, more popularly known as Wat Pho. 'Wat' is the Thai word for a temple and Wat Pho is probably Thailand's most important temple.

Wat Pho is really a large complex with a number of shrines and a monastery next to the Grand Palace. It is especially well known to tourists because of its statue of a reclining Buddha and because of its museum. The whole place is glorious. Built in the eighteenth century, it has steeply pitched roofs of brightly coloured tiles, walls inset with pieces of mirror, monuments with coloured porcelain in the shapes of flowers and gilt spires all shining in the sun. Wat Pho was Thailand's first university and it is still the national headquarters for the teaching and preservation of traditional Thai medicine.

So, there is much to be seen and visitors can also have a traditional Thai massage or take a Thai massage course .

I had been to Wat Pho as a tourist many times over the years but on one particular Sunday, about six or seven years ago, I had gone there to say my prayers. I was sitting on the floor of one of the smaller shrines. Thais sit cross-legged. I can't. I've tried and it just doesn't work. In Thailand it is rude to sit with your feet sticking out in front and as there were no chairs in the temple, legs to one side it was.

I had just settled into this position when along came a monk, actually a novice, about seventeen years old. He sat on the floor beside me.

'Hello, where you from?'

'New Zealand,' I answered.

Then, after a little pause, he said, 'Do you speak English?'

I said that I did and he asked if he could practise his English on me. I said that he could if he would just give me a few minutes to finish what I was doing. After that we could have an English lesson. He seemed very happy with that and went off to reappear about ten minutes later.

I don't think he learnt much from me but I certainly learned a lot from him, both then and in the years that followed, for we kept in touch.

His name is Panom. Panom had been a monk since he was thirteen, at first in a monastery to the west of Bangkok and then, encouraged by a teacher, he moved to Wat Pho for more education. When I first met him, he was just beginning university with one of the first groups of Thai Buddhist monks to go to an ordinary university. Many monks had been to university before but only to religious ones. Panom was to attend the state university, Mahidol

University where he was to study world religions, philosophy, English and business management.

He told me about his day. It began at 4.00am and included long periods of academic study and lectures, many of them in English. It took him an hour and a half to get to the university by public transport and the same time to return. In addition, there was his usual cycle of meditation and other religious duties, including the early morning walk through the streets with his bowl to receive the food offerings of the faithful. He would never eat after midday. That is the rule for Buddhist monks, and he went to bed about 11.00pm. What a day! The weekends, too, were well occupied for he taught children about Buddhism in the temple's Sunday school.

Panom and I kept in touch, usually by e-mail. His English needed a certain amount of attention and over the years I tried to help. I was, though, rather mystified by one of his early e-mails:

'I wish for your family very happiness.'

Well, the 'very' was probably a typing error and clearly he had meant 'every happiness'. But then it continued, 'and for you I hope, funny your works.'

Now, I like the idea of having 'funny my works' but could I work out what he meant? Eventually, my younger son said, 'But Dad, it's obvious. Think!'

I thought, and it wasn't obvious at all.

'Oh come on,' he said. 'Funny- fun- enjoy! Works- work! He's saying that he hopes you are enjoying your work.'

And he was too. A pity in a way. I preferred, 'for you I hope funny your works.'

I once asked Panom if there was something I could bring him. I was on my way to England and later I would be coming back to New Zealand through Bangkok. I thought he might like some English textbooks or something like that.

Rather shyly, he said, 'Yes, there is something I would like.'

'Good!' I said. 'What is it?'

'Only if it is easy for you to get.'

'Of course, but what?'

'Could you get me, please, a Manchester United Football Club scarf?'

In Thailand! In that heat! With saffron robes! A monk, a serious student of theology and a football fan as well.

only a camera

Of course sometimes it's a bit of a nightmare travelling on the tube with signal failures, trains breaking down, and the heat. Still, I enjoy it not just because it gets me from A to B but because of the chance it gives me just to observe the others in the carriage. No doubt it also gives others the chance to observe me observing the others. You don't usually talk to people on the tube but New Zealanders seem to be able to get away with many things, even talking on the underground.

The other day I realized that the young woman sitting next to me had a sketch pad out and was quietly drawing portraits of others in the carriage. She became aware that I was watching her and looked a bit embarrassed, so I said quietly, pointing to one sketch, 'You've really caught him there.' And she had and she was pleased that I had recognized her skill in capturing the likeness of this stranger sitting opposite.

About a year or more ago, I was on another tube journey, from Notting Hill Gate. Sitting opposite me were three Arab women not only wearing the 'chador' which covers them from head to foot and includes a veil over the lower part of their faces, but they were also wearing strange, almost frightening masks often made of leather but this time shaped from metal - large metal spectacles leaving only two slits through which to see but not be seen. The anonymity of the wearer was assured. The mask was disfiguring. Its purpose was achieved.

Along from me was a black American woman tourist. Clearly fascinated by the Arab women, she took out her camera to photograph them. The moment the three women saw what she was doing they turned away in horror and a man who I hadn't even realized was with them, got up and stood between the Arab women and the American saying, 'No! No!'

The American woman smiled. 'It's OK. It's only a camera.'

'No!' said the man beginning to get angry. 'No!'

The photographer was totally bewildered and I said to her quietly, 'Put your camera away.'

'But why?'

'Put it away!' I said. And she did.

I tried to explain to her that for these Muslim women to be photographed, to have their image captured, was deeply offensive.

'But why?' she again repeated. How could I explain that for some, the commandment, 'Thou shalt not take unto thyself any graven image nor the likeness of anything in the heavens above or in the earth beneath or in the water under the earth,' means absolutely no images, no paintings and no photos.

And this happened before the Taliban utterly destroyed the Buddha images that had been in the central Bamiyan Valley in Afghanistan since the sixth century, because they found those images offensive.

And in the 16th century, Thomas Cromwell and his soldiers rode their horses into English cathedrals and lopped the heads off the medieval statues because they found them offensive.

These days of course we know better. We know that we must respect the culture and beliefs of others. We believe in personal freedom. But it is not always that easy when we see that one person's freedom to take a photo destroys another person's freedom not to be photographed.

those precious cups of meaning

I tried to contact an airline by phone. It was to do with my flight from Christchurch to Melbourne. As usual, I listened to a recorded message and had to push a number of buttons before I could even get going.

'Your call is important to us. A customer service agent will be with you shortly.' Their 'customer service agent'? After I had heard this eleven times, it soon became apparent that my call was not important at all. They were saving money on the number of 'customer service agents' and I, their 'valued' customer, was receiving no service.

On another occasion, the system was even more elaborate. There were four recorded messages. The first – 'We appreciate your call. A team member will be with you as soon as they can.' Music. Then the second – 'Thank you for calling us today. We will be with you as quickly as we can.' This was followed by - 'We appreciate your taking time to call us today. We are working on connecting your call.' And finally, 'Welcome. Thanks for calling. We'll be with you as soon as we can.' It was no surprise when it then went back to – 'We appreciate your……..'

These systems are now in operation all over the world. You hear what appears to be the same concerned voice and virtually the same message whether you are in London, Bangkok, Kuala Lumpur, Sydney or Auckland.

But at the end of my call to the airline I eventually did get a person, only to discover that my flight had been 'rescheduled'. That meant - cancelled.

Those recorded messages have turned me into an unbeliever. No longer do I believe that airlines 'appreciate' my calls. Nor do I believe that words such as 'soon', 'quickly', or 'service' can be trusted to have the meaning they once had for me.

And with those recorded telephone messages, we have come a long way from St Augustine saying, 'Words, those precious cups of meaning.'

Those words on the telephone recordings don't mean a thing.

queen's birthday at the embassy

I read in a newspaper about a tea party on the lawn at the British Embassy in Kabul, Afghanistan. Surely, tea on a lawn is no big deal at a British Embassy? But this time it was a bit different – there were no cucumber sandwiches because there wasn't a cucumber to be found in Kabul in 2001. The Taliban had not long been gone so they made do with chopped up hard-boiled egg sandwiches, tuna pate sandwiches, and sponge cake.

The event was to honour two men, Zahoor Shah and Afzal Syed. They were being rewarded for their devotion to duty, each receiving an honorary MBE. And the duty? They had been members of the staff of the Embassy since they were employed as tennis ball boys at the age of 8 and 9. Now in their late fifties they were still at the Embassy where for 23 years of their employment they had been the only staff. At the time of the Russian invasion these two stayed on and when the British abandoned the embassy in 1989, the last diplomat taking the union flag with him, civil war loomed. Not only did these two stay, they went through the Embassy secretly, hiding anything of value. They hid two full-length portraits of Queen Mary and King George the fifth under a broken bed in an attic. They hid the Wilton china and the silver tea service embossed with the British coat of arms. They hid crystal glasses and silver teaspoons. Regularly, over the years they checked that everything was safe and they slept in the gatehouse determined to repel intruders.

In 1996 a rocket plunged into the compound killing a carpenter and still these two carried on. When the Taliban came to power later that year they stayed.

'You have performed a remarkable service over many years,' Ronald Nash, Britain's new Ambassador to Afghanistan, told them in his speech at the tea party.

'Today we are here to pay tribute to you. You have worked faithfully to protect our embassy. There has been physical danger and war around you and for many years you have taken care of our possessions when there was no British ambassador and there were no British officials. We know that life has been difficult for you and your families throughout all this time,' he said as a lone piper played Scotland the Brave and Land of Hope and Glory and the guests sipped their tea.

Mr Shah said, 'The British have always been very good to me. I have served them faithfully and will continue to do so.'

Mr Syed said, 'For 13 years the embassy was closed altogether, but I did not allow anyone to pass. Once the Taliban asked us to let them in and asked what was there. I told them just a few old tables and chairs and they went away.' Then he said he was honoured that the Queen had given him a medal, adding, 'I will work here until I'm fired. When someone at the embassy says I must stop, I will stop.'

For Mr Shah and Mr Syed an honour – for duty and for loyalty.

trampling the crocuses

I sat one morning in London's Kennington Park, south of the river, enjoying the early spring sunshine, the freshness in the air and the crocuses in bloom, when I saw a young man coming towards me along the path. Obviously wanting to get to the gate by a short cut, he walked straight through the crocuses – trampling them without thought. It wasn't even as if he seemed angry with life and was making a point. I could have understood that. No. He just wanted to get to the gate, so he crushed the crocuses on the way. I was about to call out, 'Hey, don't walk on the crocuses,' or something like that. Then I stopped and thought, 'I don't want to get punched in the face.'

Not long after this, I was talking to a retired senior civil servant, a man who had reached the top of his profession, respected and perhaps even a little feared within his department. He told me that he had been on a bus and some young people, racketing about, had knocked into an old lady and nearly sent her flying. Not malicious, just badly behaved. 'I was going to tell them to stop and then I thought, 'Dare I? And I didn't, so I said nothing.'

And then I was standing in a queue at an airport. The baggage x-ray machines weren't working so that people were lining up all over the place. In front of me was an elderly, not especially tall, not especially imposing Englishman. A young tourist pushed into the line in front of the Englishman and stood there. The Englishman lent forward and said, quite quietly and very politely, 'Excuse me, people are queuing.'

And the young man replied, 'You can f… off.'

Then the Englishman said, 'Actually, it's not a matter of 'f……' it's a matter of queuing.

The young man went to the back of the queue. We all clapped.

KENNINGTON

first catch your fish

I'm sure Mrs Beeton began one of her recipes, 'First catch your fish.....'

As children, we used to walk against the flow of the water in one of the streams beside the main road that went through the farm in South Canterbury. The aim was to catch trout. First, you'd spot a trout, tickle along its body, then fingers in the gills, catch it. I know that if a car went by we'd duck down so as not to be seen. Tickling trout is illegal. It's unfair on the trout.

Once, when I was in a small rural village in north east Thailand I went fishing. Well, really a whole extended family went on a picnic and they included me. About twenty of us piled onto a trailer pulled by a small tractor and set off through the light bush to the paddy fields. The rice had been harvested and anyway we were going fishing.

In the corner of some of the paddy fields there were

fishponds, small man-made ponds, and we settled near one of these. A petrol pump was unloaded and put together. One end of a wide flexible pipe was attached to the pump. The other was put into the pond.

All this took a bit of time but we drank the local beer, someone lit a fire and we watched as the pump didn't start, then did start and stopped, and then started again. It was all fairly usual stuff with pumps.

Eventually, when the pump worked, the pond was drained of water. It was simply pumped out into the dry paddy field. The fish here were catfish and they appeared to live in the mud. It was all very straightforward. When the pond was empty you got in. The mud came up to your thighs.

Then you caught the fish with your hands and threw them into a basket. There was a rather clever arrangement at the top so that once they were in, the fish couldn't jump out again. If your feet slip doing this you end up covered in mud. But it's hot, the mud is cool and everyone laughs a lot.

After fishing this pond, we moved onto a second where there were snakefish. At this pond the system was different. We still used the pump, but this time I noticed that a net had been put below the outlet of the pump. It was simple really. Simple, effective fishing. You started the pump and pumped out the water and the fish. The fish landed in the net. You gutted them, well actually I didn't, speared them with a bamboo cane, grilled them over the fire, then ate them. Delicious!

When I suggested that this mightn't be fair, I was looked at in complete amazement and some bewilderment.

'Not fair to whom?'

'To the fish,' I said.

'But they're fish!' was the amazed response. 'Fish, for food.'

And they were, and very good too.

The odd thing is that though everything I experienced on that farm in Esarn, north eastern Thailand was totally different from anything I'd ever known before - the people, the language, the clothes, the paddy fields and the jungle, there was also something deeper that was incredibly familiar.

It took me back to my childhood, to New Zealand, to South Canterbury, to my home and to the farm. In a way it could all just as easily have been a picnic from my childhood when, on a hot summer day, a whole lot of us would pile into the back of a truck and go up the Rangitata gorge. We would stop by a stream at the willows, unpack a picnic and cook over an open fire.

But of course we would never have fished with a petrol pump.

hello where are you from?

I met three Buddhist monks when I was walking around the Shwe Dagon Pagoda, Myanmar/Burma's most sacred shrine. I find Buddhist monks in their saffron robes and with shaven heads and eyebrows, striking, enigmatic figures, and to say that ' I met' them may be going too far but one of the good things about travelling on your own is that people come up and talk to you. When you're with someone else or in a tour group, it just doesn't happen.

I did have a guide to the Shwe Dagon but I'd left her at the entrance because I just wanted to wander. Anyway, the first monk who said 'hello' was in his early thirties.

'Hello, where you from?' It's the unvarying first question.

'New Zealand.'

'Ah, Switzerland.'

'No. New Zealand. New Zealand!' Then, reluctantly I'm

afraid, 'New Zealand, near Australia.' From then on the conversation can go in almost any direction.

This monk wanted to make quite sure I had the right view of Buddhism. As our conversation continued, what really struck me was the similarity of his approach to that of certain Christians, Jews and Muslims that I had met at different times in different countries around the world. And not only religious people but members of political parties and social movements.

He was someone who knew what was right, what was true and what was what. And he wanted to make sure that I had got it right as well. As a style, I must admit it puts me off rather than encouraging me but he was interesting. He had become a monk in his early twenties and was obviously intelligent and committed – probably a 'high flyer'. He had made vows for life.

Not all Buddhist monks make life vows. Most Buddhist males at some time in their lives enter the monkhood perhaps for just a month. For many, especially those from poor families, part of their education will be to spend time as a boy monk in a school attached to a temple. There are comparatively few Buddhist nuns.

Businessmen whose businesses collapse or who have a disaster at work, will enter the monkhood to get their spiritual balance back or to have a sort of spiritual clean out or to atone for what has gone wrong. The driver of the taxi I used had a shaven head – not for fashion. He had had a month in the monkhood because he'd been ill and wanted to get spiritually as well as physically well. He was to be married in a few weeks he told me and a month at a temple seemed a good way to prepare for that as well.

'Hello, where you from?' said the second monk I met at the Shwe Dagon. He was in his seventies and he told me he had been a monk for only a few years. His wife had died, his children were grown up 'and now', he said, 'I have found peace.' It was obvious that he had. He was a figure of total serenity. He and I spent as much time sitting silently next to each other as we did talking.

My third monk never spoke to me at all. As I walked around I became aware of a small figure following me at a distance of probably five metres or so. I guess he was eight or nine years old, rather solemn. He was just there, following and watching me - a boy - a monk.

I don't know why he followed me. I'm over six feet tall and that's unusual for Burma. I'm European and fair-haired but I don't think that can have been it. Anyway, he never left me.

When the time came for me to go, I left the Shwe Dagon and met my guide and the taxi with the shaven headed taxi driver. As we were moving off I saw the littlest monk just standing there, so I waved. His face lit up like the sun. A huge grin went from ear to ear. And he waved and waved. And I waved until he was out of sight.

the dirty old man

Bangkok's sky train is a bit like the London underground, only instead of being below ground it is elevated above the streets. The proper name for it is the 'Bangkok Rapid Transit System'. And that is just what it is, for it is fast, it gets you efficiently to where you want to go and it is air-conditioned which in Bangkok's heat is exactly what you want. But none of that is really the point.

One morning, I was sitting in the train when an elderly man, an American, a retired teacher as it turned out, got on. He was dressed in t-shirt, shorts and sandals. Thais would not consider this to be correct dress for town but tourists seem to get away with more or less anything. There were no more seats so the man, along with a number of others, was standing, holding onto a strap.

Finding himself next to a young Thai woman, the man turned to her and said, 'You look very beautiful today.'

The young woman, who was indeed beautiful, answered, 'Thank you very much.'

The man told her he was from Florida and that he was retired. He then went on to question the young woman and some of the questions became quite personal. She answered them all, charmingly and politely.

He then turned to another young woman, 'You are very pretty,' he said. She too, answered politely. After we had been travelling for about five minutes he had used more or less the same line on five young women. All were Thai. All spoke politely to him. One apologised for not speaking English.

Of course, politeness is the Thai way and I realised that the most any Thai would say in the face of what had struck me as embarrassing pick up lines would be, 'You have a sweet mouth,' which I suppose translates as, 'You flatterer.' That is as much of a put down as a Thai would use.

I caught the eye of another tourist. He was clearly as fascinated by the conversations as I was and we raised our eyes heavenwards in disbelief and some discomfort at the behaviour of our fellow tourist. I was thinking how the same approach would have gone down in London, Miami, or Auckland and decided that by now he would have been told to 'back off', possibly in no uncertain terms.

As the elderly American began his line on yet another young woman, I thought the whole thing was beginning to become fairly unpleasant. 'You dirty old man!' I thought. Just then the train came into a railway station and the man said to the young women, 'Thank you. It's been so nice talking to you. I am alone. It is nice to talk to someone. Thank you for being so kind.' He got out and we were all left to continue our journey. I realised that he may have been a bit eccentric but the evil thoughts were in my mind. They were not in his.

robbed in rio de janeiro

I was robbed in Rio de Janeiro. Well everyone is robbed in Rio de Janeiro. I'd been told that, so I knew to be careful. I'd been out to dinner with friends, really nice and relaxed, casual, no jackets or ties. They were going on somewhere else but I was a bit tired. I would go back to the apartment and get an early night if that was alright. They asked if I was sure I'd be OK and I said, 'Of course.'

The apartment was only three blocks away, in a respectable part of town with well lit streets and all the rest of it. So, there I was, walking along a perfectly safe street. I took a short cut down a slightly quieter street and strolled along, happy and rather mellow after a pleasant dinner. Suddenly, there in front of me was a very large man. I thought he was going to ask me the way. What a pity I didn't speak Portuguese. I needn't have worried, 'Mafia do Brazil,' the large man said. Then, in perfect English, 'Give me money!'

I didn't hesitate. He was much bigger than me. I was putting my hands to my trouser pockets when to my great surprise two hands from someone behind me got there first, flicked out my money and within seconds both the big man in front and his accomplice behind, small or large I don't know, were gone.

I continued walking and put my hands into my pockets. My handkerchief was still there, and my credit card and the keys to the apartment. Only the money, barely twenty five dollars, was gone. I felt strangely grateful. Here I was totally unharmed, still with the key, still with my credit card and I had had an interesting experience. Of course, it could have been worse. He could have had a knife. I could have been beaten up. But he didn't have a knife and it wasn't worse.

Then something I had been thinking about lately became clearer. I understood for the first time why some governments, before a new budget, leak out the news of how tough that budget is going to be. Then, when it is announced and isn't nearly as bad as you feared, you actually feel quite grateful.

But however grateful I was in that street in Rio, I knew I had still been robbed.

the temple of the golden buddha

The Temple of the Golden Buddha, Wat Traimit, is one of Thailand's most visited tourist sites. It is not far from Bangkok's main railway station – about five minutes walk, a bit tricky to find but the locals are used to tourists looking for it and they're most helpful at showing the way. The temple itself is not especially distinguished. It was built as recently as 1955 but the Buddha image it contains has always been venerated by the Thai people. For a start it is old, more than seven hundred years old, and it was brought from the north to a quite different temple in Bangkok on the other side of town. It was moved to Wat Traimit in 1931.

But only in 1955 did the tourists become really interested. The then abbot decided to have the Buddha image moved to a new building he had had especially constructed for it. The image was big – about sixteen feet tall and heavy, so it took some moving. In the process of being moved, the image cracked and the gold leaf covered plaster of the image was partly broken. Only then, was it discovered that underneath the plaster was another image of solid gold, the largest gold Buddha image in the world, twelve feet five inches in diameter, fifteen feet nine inches tall and weighing about five tons. Five tons of solid gold!

This very beautiful image of the Buddha subduing Mara, came from a time when Sukothai was the capital of Thailand, a time that some would consider Thai art to be at its height. It had been covered with another image in plaster to protect it from enemies invading Thailand more than half a century before. An image hidden within an image. Hidden for a purpose. Hidden for survival. Captured, it would have been melted down and destroyed.

In Tiffanys, the jewellers in New York, I gather they sell hollow gold bangles. But there's something inside the hollow so that if you shake one it rattles. You are told that inside the bangle there are some diamonds. You can't see them but you can hear them and if you buy one of these bangles you certainly pay for the diamonds as well as for the gold. So you have to trust Tiffany's. And should someone give you a bangle with a rattle you would have to trust the giver and believe that there were diamonds inside. You do, of course, have the option of destroying the bangle and having a look.

These days, we seem to think that we must always see what is inside things – inside institutions, inside government departments and inside other people – what they think and what they believe. It's called 'openness' or 'transparency'. Nothing is to be left hidden; all is probed, analysed or discussed; the mystery is destroyed and the diamonds lost.

Years ago, I had to conduct a seminar on human relationships and I asked a wise, older priest to help me. 'Oh no, Simon, you don't want me,' he said.

‘Yes, I do,’ I said, ‘or I wouldn’t have asked you.’

‘I won’t be any good. You’re going to tell everyone to ‘let it all hang out’ and I’m going to tell them to tuck it all back in again.’

I wonder what all those western tourists are seeing when they get to Wat Traimit, the Temple of the Golden Buddha. Are they seeing a stunningly beautiful Sukothai period work of art? Are they seeing an image of the founder of Buddhism that inspires meditation on his teaching? Or do we perhaps just go to look at five tons of solid gold?

the christmases of my childhood

The Christmases of my childhood were quite wonderful. The sun shone and we were happy.

The shape of our Christmas Day never changed. I don't know where this particular pattern came from but clearly it was the right pattern because it was ours. We had pillowcases for our presents. We would put the pillowcases at the ends of our beds on Christmas Eve and when we awoke on Christmas Day we would check out the others' pillowcases to see whose was the fullest. Well I did, so I assume the others did the same.

Then we all dragged our pillow cases into our parents' bedroom, fought over who could get into bed with them, the youngest always won, and opened our presents. Next on the agenda, church. Totally familiar service, totally familiar hymns, total bliss. One lot of neighbours who came to church were not allowed to open their presents until after the service. We thought that very peculiar.

Cousins from Timaru would arrive before Christmas dinner and then there were one or two others because my mother said, 'You always behave better if there's someone who's not family.' And of course she was right.

The highlight of Christmas dinner was the Christmas pudding. One of my brothers would draw the curtains so that it was dark for my father to spoon the burning brandy over the holly on the pudding. And my mother would say, 'That was so beautiful, you must do it again.' And we knew she would say it, and she did. And my father would do it again, heating the brandy in an old spoon over a candle, then when it caught fire he would put out the candle with his left hand - fingers licked first - and over the holly, blue and yellow flames would dance for the second time. I've never been crazy on Christmas pudding but I loved the ceremony.

After our Christmas dinner, more visitors would arrive, including the family with the strange present opening habits, and we would play 'Kick the Tin'. We were wonderfully lucky for our home had a garden with excellent hiding places – a jumble of japonica on what must have once been a rubbish dump, a huge Lawsoniana, later to be cut down because it took the sun off the house in the afternoon and a Wellingtonia at the bottom of the garden which was good to hide behind, though a bit far from the tin unless you had a very clear run.

At four o'clock, Father Christmas arrived. He always said, 'Ho, Ho, Ho', and gave everyone small, fun presents as we stood around the Christmas tree in the hall. He seemed to us children to be strangely familiar with rather proper, elderly guests. The evening meal was very simple. Scrambled eggs. The sun shone. We were happy.

Some years ago, I was talking with the family about these Christmases and my father said that sometimes it had rained on Christmas Day. I said it hadn't – not ever. He looked it up in the farm diaries. From when I was four until I was eighteen it had rained on more Christmas days than not. And, my mother added, on every one of those Christmas days there had been some sort of a family row. Frequently, she said, I had spent some of the time sulking and would then end up hiding in the dirty clothes basket in the wash house.

Is what I remember untrue? The record is clear. It rained. There were rows. What has happened to the sun and my happiness? Truly, the Christmases of my childhood were wonderful. We were happy and the sun shone.